MAYER SMITH

The Echoes of a Fallen Star

Contents

1 The Night of the Falling Star   1

2 The Awakening   7

3 Shadows in the Light   15

4 The Prophecy's First Mark   23

5 The Whispers   29

6 A Kiss Against Destiny   36

7 The Betrayal Foretold   43

8 The Celestial Hunt   50

9 A Star's Desperate Plea   57

10 Fall   64

11 Echoes   70

12 The Heart of the Storm   77

One

The Night of the Falling Star

The storm came without warning.

One moment, the sky above Solace Bay was a calm, inky black, the crescent moon silvering the restless waves. The next, clouds thickened like ink spilled into water, rolling over the coastline with a force that made the air electric. Elara Vale tightened her grip on the wrought-iron balcony railing, the salt-laden wind tangling her long, auburn hair.

She had seen storms before—felt their anger in the way the ocean churned, tasted their raw power in the metallic air before the first drop of rain fell. But this was different. The pressure in the atmosphere didn't just promise rain. It felt like the sky itself was holding its breath.

Then she saw it.

A light—brighter than anything she had ever seen—tore through the heavens. It wasn't like a shooting star, those fleeting streaks of silver that danced across the night sky. No, this was a blazing inferno, streaking through the darkness like something falling, breaking, burning.

It was impossibly fast, yet she could see every detail—the way the fire curled at its edges, flickering blue and gold, the trail of molten embers raining down in its wake. Her heart pounded against her ribs, an instinctual warning screaming at her to run, to hide—

But she couldn't move.

She was entranced.

The star—or whatever it was—was coming down fast, and it was heading straight for the cliffs on the outskirts of town.

A deafening boom ripped through the night as it struck earth. The ground beneath her trembled, a shockwave rolling through Solace Bay like an earthquake, shaking windows and rattling wind chimes. In the distance, a pillar of golden fire surged skyward, illuminating the cliffside with an eerie glow before it flickered and dimmed.

Elara's breath came in sharp, uneven gasps.

Something inside her—something she did not understand— lurched forward, pulling her like a tide toward the wreckage.

She didn't think. She just moved.

The cliffs loomed ahead, jagged and ominous against the backdrop of the turbulent sea. Elara's boots skidded on the damp, uneven ground as she ran, her pulse hammering in time with each frantic step.

She should have called someone. The police. Scientists. Anyone. But her mind rejected logic, leaving only a single, unshakable truth—

She needed to see it for herself.

Lightning forked across the sky, illuminating the smoking crater carved into the earth. The impact had splintered the cliffside, rock jutting at unnatural angles, the scent of scorched earth and ionized air thick in her lungs. The crash site pulsed with a dim, ethereal light, golden veins running through the fractured stone like liquid fire.

And at its center—

Someone was there.

Elara's breath hitched.

A man lay in the hollowed earth, half-buried in the scorched remains of the fallen star. His body was lean, almost too perfectly sculpted, draped in what looked like dark, tattered fabric that shimmered strangely in the dim light. His skin, though smudged with soot, gleamed like it had been carved from moonlight itself.

His chest rose and fell in ragged, shallow breaths. He was alive.

Elara took an unsteady step forward, her body thrumming with a strange energy, as if the very air had changed around her.

And then his eyes opened.

A violent shockwave of awareness slammed into her, knocking the breath from her lungs.

His eyes were unlike anything she had ever seen—not human, not earthly. The irises were a swirling mix of gold and obsidian, shifting and pulsing like distant galaxies trapped within them. For a fraction of a second, she swore she saw stars burning in their depths, constellations forming and unraveling in a blink.

Then pain overtook his features. He groaned, trying to move, but his body was too weak.

Elara swallowed hard, forcing herself to push past her shock.

"You're hurt," she whispered, dropping to her knees beside him. She had no idea what he was, but right now, he was suffering. And something inside her—something deep and unshakable— refused to leave him like this.

She reached out, fingertips hovering just above his bare skin.

The moment they touched—

A surge of blinding, golden light erupted between them.

It wasn't just light. It was heat. Power. It roared through her veins, stealing her breath, forcing her eyes shut as a thousand fragments of memory flooded her mind—visions of worlds unknown, burning constellations, a voice calling her name across time and space.

She wrenched her hand away with a startled gasp, her heart slamming against her ribs.

The man—if he was even that—was staring at her, wide-eyed, breathing heavily.

"You…" His voice was rough, like it hadn't been used in centuries. His gaze flickered over her, intense, calculating, like he recognized her. Like he had been waiting for her.

Elara swallowed hard, her hands trembling.

"What—" Her voice faltered. She tried again. "What are you?"

He exhaled slowly, still watching her with an unreadable expression.

Then, finally, he whispered—

"I am the last of the fallen. And now… you are bound to me."

A gust of wind rushed through the crater, carrying the scent of burning stardust.

Elara's stomach clenched with something both terrifying and exhilarating.

She had come searching for a falling star.

But she had found something else entirely.

Something that had already changed her forever.

Two

The Awakening

Elara woke with a start.

A sharp, breathless gasp tore from her throat as she shot upright, her body drenched in sweat. Her heart hammered against her ribs, a frantic, disoriented rhythm. For a moment, she had no idea where she was—only the lingering sensation of blinding golden light coursing through her veins, the phantom heat still burning beneath her skin.

The crater. The fallen star. The man—

Her breath hitched.

She wasn't on the cliffs anymore. She was in her bedroom, surrounded by the familiar scent of rain-soaked wood and sea salt drifting in through the open window. The sheets tangled around her legs, damp with perspiration.

Had it been a dream?

No.

She could feel it. A strange, residual energy coiled deep in her chest, pulsing faintly beneath her ribs like a second heartbeat. She pressed a trembling hand to her sternum, her fingertips tingling with something unfamiliar.

The memory slammed into her—

The stranger's impossible eyes, dark as obsidian but burning with galaxies. The way his skin had been cool to the touch despite the fire surrounding him. The connection that had flared the instant their hands met, as if something ancient and unseen had locked them together in a bond neither of them understood.

And his final words before everything went dark:

"I am the last of the fallen. And now… you are bound to me."

Elara shuddered, drawing her knees to her chest.

The storm had passed, leaving behind an eerie silence. Beyond her window, the ocean stretched into the horizon, its surface unnaturally still, as if the entire world was holding its breath. The town of Solace Bay was quiet, save for the occasional creak of a boat rocking in the distant harbor.

But something felt off.

A whisper of unease curled around the edges of her thoughts.

And then—

A shadow moved across her window.

Elara froze.

Her breath caught in her throat as she stared at the figure outside—tall, unmoving, silhouetted against the faint glow of the streetlamp.

He found me.

The moment the thought crossed her mind, the figure moved. Slowly. Deliberately.

Elara's pulse thundered. Every muscle in her body tensed as she scrambled off the bed, fumbling for something—anything—to use as a weapon. Her hands found the heavy glass lamp on her nightstand.

The figure stepped forward.

She swung.

The lamp shattered against the hardwood floor as a hand shot out and caught her wrist mid-strike.

"Elara."

The sound of her name, spoken in that voice, sent a tremor through her entire body.

She looked up—

And her breath stalled.

It was him.

Orion.

His dark, celestial eyes bore into hers, their depths unreadable. He stood in her room as if he had always belonged there— towering, otherworldly, his presence sending a ripple of unease through the very air. His black clothing was still scorched from the impact, his skin pale beneath the golden residue of fading stardust.

"Elara," he repeated, his grip on her wrist firm but not painful. "You're different."

Different.

The word sent a chill racing down her spine.

She yanked free of his grasp, stumbling back, her pulse a wild, erratic drumbeat in her ears. "How—how are you here? What the hell is going on?"

He exhaled slowly, his gaze flickering over her, as if he were seeing something inside her, something even she couldn't sense. "You felt it, didn't you?"

Elara swallowed hard. "Felt what?"

"The bond."

The moment the word left his lips, something inside her twisted.

She didn't want to believe it. Didn't want to acknowledge the truth that had already settled deep in her bones. But she couldn't ignore the pull, the invisible thread that tethered her to him, an energy humming beneath her skin that hadn't been there before.

"What did you do to me?" she whispered.

Orion's expression darkened. "It wasn't me," he murmured. "It was the star."

Elara shivered.

A thousand questions fought to spill from her lips, but her mind latched onto the one that mattered most.

"Why do I feel like…" She hesitated, searching for the words. "Like something inside me has… changed?"

Orion studied her for a long moment, then stepped closer.

She didn't move.

The distance between them disappeared in an instant, and for a second, Elara forgot how to breathe.

"You weren't meant to touch me," he murmured. His voice was lower now, softer, but edged with something dangerous.

A warning.

"But you did." His gaze dropped to her hands. "And now, part of the star's power flows through you."

A sharp chill spread through her veins.

"You're saying I absorbed… whatever it was?"

"Yes."

Panic coiled around her ribs. "And what does that mean?"

Orion's jaw tightened. A flicker of something unreadable passed through his features before he answered.

"It means you've become part of something… irreversible."

The weight of those words settled heavily between them.

Elara's breath came in shallow, uneven pulls. "I don't want to be part of this," she said, her voice barely above a whisper. "I just want my life back."

Orion's expression softened—just slightly.

"I wish that were possible," he admitted. "But the moment you touched me… your fate was rewritten."

The finality in his tone sent ice through her veins.

She took a shaky step back.

"No," she murmured. "There has to be a way to undo this."

"There isn't."

The words were simple, but they shattered something inside her.

Elara shook her head, anger and fear clashing in her chest. "Then why are you here? What do you want from me?"

Orion hesitated.

Then, almost reluctantly, he said, "To keep you alive."

A chill ran down her spine.

"Alive?" she echoed.

Orion's gaze darkened, shadows flickering behind those celestial eyes.

"There are forces that will come for you now," he said quietly.

"Beings that will sense the power inside you. They will want to claim it." He paused. "And they will destroy you to get it."

The air in the room suddenly felt too thin.

Elara's fingers curled into fists. She should have been terrified. She should have been running, screaming, demanding answers.

But deep inside her, beneath the fear and uncertainty…

A part of her already knew.

Something had awakened in her on that cliffside.

And now, there was no going back.

Three

Shadows in the Light

The world felt off.

It wasn't just the way the air around Elara crackled, like an invisible current was running beneath the surface of reality. It wasn't just the way her skin tingled, hypersensitive, every nerve on edge like she was hearing a sound too high-pitched for human ears.

It was something deeper.

Like a thread had been pulled from the fabric of her life, unraveling something unseen, something she could feel but not name.

She pressed a hand to her chest, her fingers trembling slightly. Since last night—since Orion's arrival, since that impossible surge of energy had shot through her—her body hadn't felt like her own.

Her senses were sharper.

The ocean outside her window sounded different, the waves carrying distant murmurs that hadn't been there before. The scent of salt, of damp stone, of storm-washed air—it was stronger, overwhelming. She could hear the slow, rhythmic flutter of a moth's wings against the glass of her bedside lamp, could make out the sound of footsteps outside long before the person reached her front porch.

It should have terrified her.

But the strangest part?

It felt natural.

Like something inside her had always been waiting for this moment.

A knock on the door nearly made her jump out of her skin.

Elara's heart lurched into her throat. She barely had time to steady herself before Orion's voice came through the door— low, controlled, yet threaded with an edge she hadn't noticed before.

"Elara."

Just hearing him say her name sent an unexplainable shiver through her.

She exhaled slowly, forcing herself to move, to act normal, even as nothing about this moment—nothing about her life anymore—was normal.

When she opened the door, Orion was there, standing too still, too quiet, his gaze sweeping over her as if searching for something.

And then he said, "You're changing."

Her stomach clenched.

She crossed her arms, feigning confidence she didn't feel. "Good morning to you too."

His lips didn't so much as twitch. "You don't feel it?"

Elara hesitated. She wasn't ready to admit that she did. That her body was humming with energy, like an over-tuned instrument waiting to snap.

"No idea what you're talking about," she lied.

Orion tilted his head slightly, studying her. His presence was unnerving—too intense, too aware. He hadn't spoken much since last night, but even in silence, his presence filled the space like an unseen force.

"Elara." His voice dropped lower. "Don't lie to me."

She swallowed hard.

How did he know?

A gust of wind rushed through the doorway, pushing past them with a sudden chill. Elara shuddered, but Orion's expression turned sharp, his gaze flicking toward the street.

Then he stepped forward, too close, his voice barely above a whisper.

"Someone is watching."

Elara's pulse jumped.

She resisted the urge to glance over her shoulder. "What?"

Orion's hand brushed against her arm—barely a touch, but the contact sent a shockwave of heat through her veins, unexpected and electric. His eyes were locked onto something beyond her, scanning the street with a look so sharp it could have cut through steel.

"I felt it before I got here." His voice was calm, but his posture was coiled, like a predator sensing danger. "We're not alone."

Elara sucked in a slow, careful breath. She tried to focus—tried to listen—but all she could hear was the distant crash of waves, the rustling of wind through the trees.

But then—

A shift.

A presence.

Something lurking at the edges of her awareness, just out of reach.

The sensation was so foreign, so unnatural, that it sent her stomach twisting in on itself. The hairs on the back of her neck rose, a primal warning she couldn't ignore.

Orion must have sensed it too.

He turned his gaze back to her, and for the first time, she saw something in his expression she hadn't expected.

Not just focus. Not just tension.

Fear.

And that terrified her more than anything.

"We need to move," he murmured.

Elara hesitated. "Where?"

"Anywhere but here."

A flicker of resistance rose in her—this was her home, her life, and he was talking like they were fugitives—but before she could protest, something changed in the air.

A shadow shifted at the far end of the street.

A figure stood beneath the streetlamp—tall, unmoving, cloaked in darkness.

The light above it flickered once.

Twice.

Then died.

Elara's breath stalled. A suffocating pressure pressed against her chest, as if the very air had thickened. She tried to focus, to make out the figure's features, but it was like looking into a void, a space where no light could exist.

Orion grabbed her wrist.

"Elara, don't look at it."

But she already had.

And the moment her gaze locked onto the shadow, it moved.

Not with footsteps. Not like something that belonged in this world.

It blurred, crossing the distance between them in the blink of an eye.

Elara's stomach dropped. Her instincts screamed at her to run, but her feet were rooted in place, frozen by something she couldn't understand.

Then Orion was in front of her.

His stance shifted, his body tense with an unnatural stillness, like he was preparing for something she couldn't see. The air between them rippled, like heat distorting pavement.

"Elara." Orion's voice was sharp, commanding. "Stay behind me."

She barely had time to react before the world exploded.

The shadow lunged, tendrils of darkness ripping through the air. Orion moved fast—too fast—his body twisting as he threw out a hand.

A shockwave of golden energy erupted from his palm, colliding with the darkness in a violent crack of force.

The air shook, windows shattered, and the shadow reeled back, a distorted, shrieking noise filling the night.

Elara stumbled, gasping as the impact rattled through her bones. Her knees nearly gave out, but Orion's hand caught her before she fell.

The shadow hissed, its shape twisting unnaturally before it retreated, disappearing into the night as fast as it had appeared.

Then—

Silence.

Orion exhaled, his grip on her tightening for just a fraction of a second before he let go. His chest rose and fell with measured control, but Elara could see it—the tension in his jaw, the weight in his eyes.

"That," she whispered, voice shaking, "wasn't human."

Orion didn't respond right away.

Then, finally, he turned to her, his expression unreadable.

"No," he said quietly.

"It wasn't."

The words settled over her like a final verdict.

This wasn't a dream.

This wasn't a mistake.

Something had followed Orion to Earth.

And now, it was hunting her too.

Four

The Prophecy's First Mark

The wind had picked up by the time they reached the edge of town, the sea now a churning expanse of foam and fury, as if the ocean itself mirrored the turmoil inside Elara. She walked with Orion through the narrow streets, each step a slow, deliberate motion, her mind a whirlwind of thoughts too tangled to make sense of.

The events of the past twenty-four hours were already pushing against the edges of her consciousness, like a flood she couldn't stop. Her body had changed in ways she couldn't explain—sharp, electric sensations running through her at the slightest touch. Her mind? Even more fragmented. The shadow from last night still clung to her thoughts, its inky presence lingering in the back of her mind, like a stain on her very soul.

But worse than that was the unease in her chest whenever she glanced at Orion.

He was walking ahead of her, his movements purposeful, but his shoulders were tense, his eyes scanning the horizon with the intensity of someone who had seen too much. And yet, he was hiding something from her.

She could feel it.

"Orion," she said, her voice quiet but urgent.

He slowed but didn't turn to face her, his gaze still fixed ahead. "What?"

"I need you to explain," she began, her throat tight. "Why was that thing after me? What did you mean by 'it's not human'? I—"

"Not here," he interrupted, his tone sharp. "This isn't the place for questions. Trust me. Just keep walking."

The command was brief, but the weight behind it made her stomach tighten.

As they reached the edge of the town, the narrow streets opened up into a larger, more secluded stretch of coastline. The cliffs here were steeper, the rocks jagged and unforgiving, like teeth biting into the earth. The air smelled different here—heavier, almost charged with a quiet tension, as though something ancient and untouchable rested just beneath the surface.

Elara followed Orion down a narrow trail, the path winding like a serpent between crumbling stone and wild brush. He didn't slow, his strides long and purposeful, leading them toward the distant lighthouse at the far end of the cliffs. She recognized the place, though she had never been there before. The lighthouse had been abandoned for years, its light long extinguished, its windows cracked from years of exposure to the storms. Yet somehow, it felt… familiar.

The air was unnervingly still as they approached, the wind no longer cutting through her like it had earlier. The world around her felt like it was holding its breath.

"Why here?" she asked, her voice barely a whisper as she caught up to him.

Orion's jaw tightened, and for a moment, the weight of his silence felt like a barrier between them. When he spoke, his voice was low, tinged with something like regret. "Because this is where it begins. This is where we find out what's really happening."

Elara frowned. "What do you mean?"

Instead of answering, he pushed open a rusted door that led them into the lighthouse. The door creaked on its hinges, a sound that echoed too loudly in the otherwise dead silence. Inside, the space was dark, the air thick with the musty scent of mildew and salt. Cobwebs hung from the beams above, and the floor beneath her feet was slick with the dampness that seeped in from the sea.

"Why bring me here?" she asked again, her unease growing with each passing second.

Orion stepped into the center of the room, his form casting a long shadow against the cracked stone walls. "Because it's the only place I can show you the truth."

He moved toward a corner where an old wooden crate sat, covered in layers of dust and sea debris. With a few quick movements, he cleared it, revealing a worn leather-bound book. He held it up, his fingers brushing the edges with reverence.

"This," he said, turning toward her, "is the prophecy."

Elara's gaze flickered to the book, then back to his face. He looked like he was grieving something. His eyes were unreadable, distant. The uncertainty in his posture was unsettling.

"The prophecy?" she repeated, feeling the weight of the word in the air between them. "The one you mentioned before?"

Orion nodded, though his eyes never left the book. "Yes. The prophecy of the Fallen Star."

He placed the book carefully on a table, opening it to a page that seemed ancient, its edges frayed and yellowed with age. The text was written in a language Elara couldn't understand, the symbols intricate and delicate, like something out of a dream— or a nightmare. She leaned in, trying to make sense of it.

But before she could get any closer, Orion spoke again. "I wish

I could tell you it's not true, but the moment that star fell to earth, the prophecy began its final count."

Elara's heart skipped a beat. "The final count?"

He nodded grimly, pointing to a symbol on the page—a depiction of a falling star, surrounded by figures locked in a deadly embrace. "The star grants power to one, but at a terrible cost. The prophecy speaks of a bond that will bind the mortal and the celestial, a bond that cannot be broken. And when that bond is complete…"

He trailed off, his gaze darkening. Elara's breath caught in her throat as she waited for him to continue. But his silence spoke louder than any words could have.

"And what happens when the bond is complete?" she asked, her voice trembling.

Orion's eyes shifted toward her, the intensity of his gaze making her feel like she was standing too close to a burning flame. "The prophecy says that one will die," he replied quietly. "And the other will be left to face the consequences of a universe that has already decided their fate."

A cold chill ran down Elara's spine. "What does that mean for me?" she whispered, her voice barely audible.

"It means," Orion said, his voice a low growl, "that everything you've ever known is about to change. And you won't be able to escape it."

A sudden gust of wind slammed against the lighthouse, making the old timbers creak and groan. Elara jumped, startled. She looked toward the cracked windows, but it wasn't the wind that had unsettled her—it was the way Orion's words had landed between them, heavy and unyielding.

The moment stretched between them, thick with the weight of unspoken truths and impossible decisions.

Then, finally, Orion turned away, his jaw tight with restraint. "There's more," he muttered under his breath. "There's always more."

Elara's gaze lingered on the book in front of her, a sense of dread settling like a stone in her stomach. The prophecy was real, and it was already beginning.

The marks were being made.

And soon, the price would be paid.

Five

The Whispers

The night felt different.

The storm had passed, but its remnants lingered in the air—the oppressive humidity, the taste of salt on the tongue, the scent of wet earth and ocean spray. Elara stood at the window of her small studio apartment, watching the waves crash against the cliffs below. The sea was turbulent, its dark surface marked by white frothy lines, as though it were trying to tell her something—something she couldn't quite understand.

And then, there was the silence.

It wasn't just the quiet of the night. It was a deeper kind of silence—a weight that pressed against her chest, making her feel like something was waiting just beyond her reach.

Her fingers twitched with a restless energy she couldn't shake. It was as though the night had been stretched thin, taut with the promise of something that was coming—something she could neither run from nor prepare for.

She turned away from the window, her eyes landing on the book of the prophecy that Orion had shown her. It rested on the small table near her bed, its pages now marked with ink smudges from when she'd spent hours reading its cryptic symbols, trying to decipher the meaning behind them. But no matter how hard she looked, no matter how many translations she attempted, the words remained as mysterious as they had when she first saw them.

She needed answers.

But she didn't know where to find them.

"Elara?"

The voice from the door made her jump.

She hadn't heard him approach. Not the faintest shift in the air, not the subtle crease of the floorboards beneath his feet. It was as though he had appeared out of thin air, just like the shadow that had nearly consumed them both the night before.

Orion stood in the doorway, his silhouette bathed in the soft glow of the hallway light. His dark hair was tousled, his features sharp and unreadable as always, but there was something different about him tonight. Something darker—like the weight of the universe had settled on his shoulders, and he wasn't sure how much longer he could carry it.

"Did I startle you?" he asked, his tone soft, but laced with an edge of something she couldn't place.

Elara swallowed and shook her head. "No. Just… thinking."

"About the prophecy?"

Her heart stuttered at the mention of it. "How did you know?"

Orion took a step into the room, his presence filling the space, making it feel both unnervingly intimate and suffocating all at once. His eyes locked onto the book on the table, his gaze darkening slightly.

"You've been trying to make sense of it," he said quietly. "I know you, Elara. You don't rest until you know the truth."

She didn't respond. Instead, she crossed the room to the table and ran her fingers over the worn edges of the book.

"I need to understand," she muttered, mostly to herself. "I need to know what this means. Why did the star fall? Why… why me?"

Orion's voice was low when he spoke again. "Because you were chosen."

The words were simple, but they hit her like a physical blow.

She turned to face him, her chest tight. "Chosen?"

He nodded, his expression unreadable. "The bond that was created between us when you touched me—it was no accident. The prophecy foretold it. The star chose you, Elara, to carry its power."

"But why?" she asked, her voice breaking despite herself. "Why me? I'm just—"

"A human," Orion finished for her. "Yes. But a human capable of holding the essence of a celestial being. A mortal destined to wield something that the universe itself has deemed worthy."

Elara shook her head, her mind a whirlwind of confusion. She didn't feel powerful. She felt lost, trapped in a reality she hadn't chosen. The world had shifted around her, and she was still trying to catch up, trying to understand the forces she was suddenly entangled in.

Her eyes locked onto his, searching for some kind of reassurance, but all she found was silence—and a sadness buried deep in his gaze.

"I don't feel special," she whispered, almost ashamed of the words.

"You are," Orion said, his voice rough, his gaze intense. He stepped closer, but stopped just out of reach, as if he knew the tension between them was already thick enough to break. "You're everything this world wasn't ready for."

The air around them crackled again, like the briefest spark of lightning in the distance.

"Do you think that's a good thing?" she asked, her voice thick with emotion. "Do you think this power will make my life better?"

Orion's lips pressed together, the lines of his face hardening. "No," he answered quietly. "It will make your life… complicated."

Before she could respond, a sound outside the window caught her attention. It was faint, almost like a whisper carried by the wind. But as soon as she heard it, a chill ran down her spine. She turned toward the window, her gaze immediately drawn to the shadow that had passed in front of the streetlamp outside.

Orion's body stiffened beside her. "Someone's here."

Elara's breath hitched. "Who?"

"I don't know," Orion replied, his voice low and cautious. "But it's not good."

Without another word, he grabbed her arm, pulling her away from the window and toward the back of the room. "Stay here. Don't make a sound."

Elara barely had time to react before he disappeared into the hallway, moving with the grace and speed of someone who had spent a lifetime running from unseen enemies. She wanted to argue, to demand that he let her help, but the urgency in his movements silenced her.

The seconds stretched on, each one filled with the weight of the unknown. The shadows outside seemed to pulse with a life of their own, shifting in ways that shouldn't have been possible. A faint sound reached her ears—footsteps, slow and deliberate, creeping closer. Elara's heart pounded as she fought to steady her breathing.

And then, as if on cue, the door creaked open.

Orion stood in the doorway, his face pale, his jaw clenched tight. Behind him stood a figure, cloaked in darkness, the outline indistinguishable but menacing. The air in the room thickened, a suffocating pressure pushing down on Elara's chest.

"Who are you?" she demanded, her voice trembling despite her efforts to sound strong.

The figure stepped forward, revealing a face that wasn't quite human—too smooth, too perfect, the features sharply defined, but hollowed out in a way that made Elara's skin crawl. Its eyes were the color of cold stone, the pupils dilated and unnatural.

"I am Lucien," the figure said, its voice a soft, soothing whisper, the kind of voice that could lure you into trusting it. "And I've come for what's mine."

Elara's stomach dropped. She didn't know what he meant, but she felt it—the danger in his words, the malice in his tone.

Before she could react, Orion stepped between them, his body tense and ready. "You shouldn't be here," he said, his voice low but filled with authority. "Leave, Lucien."

Lucien tilted his head, his lips curving into a smile that didn't reach his eyes. "Oh, Orion. You've always been a stubborn one. But you're too late. The prophecy has already begun. The time for hiding is over."

The tension in the room grew unbearable, the air electric with the promise of a battle neither of them could avoid. Elara's heart raced, her instincts screaming at her to run, but she didn't know where to go. She didn't know who to trust.

And then Lucien's gaze shifted to her, and Elara felt it—a whisper in her mind, a voice that wasn't her own. "You're mine, Elara. You just don't know it yet."

Six

A Kiss Against Destiny

Elara didn't move.

The words Lucien had spoken echoed in her mind, reverberating like the clash of distant thunder. You're mine, Elara. You just don't know it yet.

She could still hear the echo of his voice in her head, smooth and insidious, a whisper that curled around her thoughts like smoke. Her heart raced as her pulse pounded in her ears. She wasn't sure whether it was the overwhelming feeling of dread that had settled into her bones or the inexplicable pull she felt when Lucien's eyes locked onto hers, but every fiber of her being screamed for her to run.

But she couldn't move.

Orion was standing between them now, his body tense, his fists clenched at his sides, his dark eyes locked onto Lucien with a fury Elara hadn't seen before. His jaw was tight, a muscle ticking in his temple as if he were holding back something primal, something dangerous.

Lucien took a slow step forward, the movement measured, deliberate. His smile never wavered, though the coldness in his eyes never left. He was like a shadow come to life, a figure born of darkness and whispers, and Elara couldn't help but feel that, just like the night, he was something that would swallow her whole if given the chance.

"Elara," Lucien said again, his voice soft but commanding, like he was speaking directly to her very soul. "You know what I'm offering you. You know that your fate is already sealed."

Elara swallowed hard, fighting the urge to back away. Her legs felt heavy, like lead weights had been placed around her ankles. Her breath came too fast, too shallow. She glanced at Orion, whose face was shadowed by something far darker than the dim light of the room. He was holding himself back, the air around him crackling with an intensity that almost made the hairs on the back of her neck stand up.

Lucien tilted his head, his gaze never leaving hers. "You could join me, Elara. You could embrace what's coming. I could give you more power than you could ever imagine. More than even Orion could offer you."

The words cut through her like a knife, and for a brief moment, she felt a flicker of something inside her—temptation. Power. She could feel it stirring deep within her, like a hidden flame just waiting to be fed. It was the same sensation that had thrummed through her veins when she'd touched Orion the night of the star's fall. But this—this was different. It wasn't the warmth she'd felt then. It was cold, calculating, like an empty promise.

"No," she whispered, her voice hoarse. "I don't want this. I don't want any of it."

Lucien's smile widened. "You're wrong. You want it more than you realize. You just need the courage to take it."

But before Elara could respond, Orion stepped forward, his eyes flashing with warning. "Stay away from her, Lucien."

For a heartbeat, there was a palpable silence between them, as if the entire room had stopped breathing. Then, with a sudden movement, Lucien let out a low chuckle, the sound almost… laughter. "I always forget how righteous you are, Orion. How you cling to your moral high ground, pretending that you can stop what's already been set in motion."

Orion's shoulders stiffened, but he didn't move. His gaze flicked toward Elara, and in that moment, something passed between them—a brief, unspoken understanding that made Elara's heart stutter in her chest. She didn't know what it was, but it felt as if the world around them had shifted ever so slightly, like a door had opened in her mind, revealing something she hadn't been able to see before.

Orion's voice was quiet, but there was an edge of raw intensity that Elara could feel all the way down to her bones. "You're wrong, Lucien. I'm not going to let you take her."

Lucien's smile faltered for a fraction of a second, but it was enough to make Elara wonder just how much he knew, how much he was hiding. "You can't stop fate, Orion. No one can. You should know that better than anyone."

With that, Lucien stepped back, his shadowy form blending seamlessly with the darkness of the room. For a brief moment, Elara thought he might leave, that he might just vanish back into the night like some nightmare, but then his gaze flicked toward her once more.

And this time, when his lips parted, there was something different in his voice—something far more chilling.

"I'll be back for you," he said, and his words seemed to hang in the air, thick and heavy, like they were imprinted into the fabric of her mind. "And when I do, you'll understand. You'll see that there is no escape."

Before she could respond, he was gone, his presence dissipating into the shadows like smoke lost in the wind.

The moment Lucien was gone, Elara's entire body seemed to exhale in a single, shaky breath she hadn't realized she'd been holding. Her heart was still pounding in her chest, her hands trembling at her sides. She felt drained, like she'd just fought an invisible battle and had barely managed to survive.

Orion didn't move right away. He stood in front of her, facing the now-empty doorway, his expression hard, unreadable. The tension in the air still hummed, thick and oppressive. She could see the muscles in his back flexing, his fists clenched at his sides as if he were fighting to contain a storm that wanted to break free.

Elara opened her mouth, but no words came out. She was shaken, still processing everything that had just happened. She had no idea who Lucien was, or why he was so intent on her. But his presence—his cold, unnerving confidence—had rattled her in a way she couldn't explain. And now, as she looked at Orion, she wondered whether she was caught between two forces that she didn't fully understand.

But the more she thought about it, the more one thing became clear: Orion wasn't the answer to everything.

Her heart thudded painfully in her chest.

Without a word, Elara stepped forward, closing the distance between them until they were only inches apart. She could feel the heat radiating from his body, the tension in the air thickening as she moved closer. Her breath hitched as their gazes locked, the weight of everything that had passed between them hanging heavy in the silence.

"Elara," Orion whispered, his voice rough, but there was something softer, more raw in it now. Something that made her pulse race even faster than before.

Before she could think, before she could stop herself, she reached up and cupped his face in her hands.

His breath hitched at the touch, his dark eyes flickering with a storm of emotions—longing, frustration, and something darker that she couldn't quite name.

And then, without another word, she kissed him.

It wasn't a soft, tentative kiss. It was a demanding kiss, a kiss that said everything they both felt, everything they hadn't been able to say aloud. The instant their lips met, a shockwave of heat surged through her, her body alive with sensation. His hands came up to grip her waist, pulling her closer as if he couldn't get close enough.

For a long moment, there was only the kiss—deep, urgent, a silent declaration of something neither of them could control. The world outside ceased to exist, and all that remained was the intensity of what they shared.

But as quickly as it had started, the kiss ended.

Orion pulled away, his chest rising and falling with heavy breaths. His eyes searched hers, his expression conflicted, as if he were fighting some inner battle.

"I can't protect you from what's coming, Elara," he murmured, his voice strained. "I'm not enough."

Elara's heart broke, the words sinking deep into her chest. She wanted to tell him he was wrong, that they could face it together. But there was something in his eyes—a fear, an ancient truth that she couldn't ignore.

Instead, she just whispered, "We'll figure it out. Together."

But even as the words left her mouth, she knew the truth.

They were already too far gone.

Seven

The Betrayal Foretold

Elara hadn't slept a wink.

The night after Lucien's warning had stretched on like a wound that wouldn't stop bleeding, every thought in her head like a jagged stone, sharp and relentless. She lay in her bed for hours, eyes wide open, staring at the ceiling. The room felt suffocating, too small for the weight of everything that had happened. Lucien's words, still echoing in her ears—You're mine, Elara. You just don't know it yet.

It had been only a day since she and Orion shared that kiss, that desperate, needful kiss. The one that had burned through her like wildfire, leaving only ashes in its wake. She didn't know where that kiss had come from, or what it meant, but it had left her with a strange emptiness that she couldn't explain. The touch of his lips still lingered on hers, like a memory she couldn't shake, yet it felt like something they had done not just out of passion, but out of necessity.

But now, in the aftermath, the tension was unbearable.

Orion hadn't spoken much since that night. His silences were becoming more frequent, his presence more distant, like a storm cloud hovering over them both. Elara could feel the pull between them, undeniable and magnetic, but it was becoming unsettling, like a thread that could snap at any moment. She tried to ignore it, tried to focus on something else—anything else—but there was no escaping it.

And now, everything was about to change.

She glanced at the clock on her nightstand. 6:00 a.m.

It was still dark outside, the sky a pale, bruised color as if it hadn't yet decided whether it was night or day. The soft sound of waves crashing against the cliffs below her apartment filled the silence, a steady rhythm that should have been calming, but now it only reminded her of how unsteady everything had become.

She stood, her feet cold against the hardwood floor, and pulled her cardigan tighter around her shoulders. The air in the room felt charged, heavy with something she couldn't quite identify, like a storm on the horizon.

A knock on the door.

Elara froze, her heart skipping a beat. It wasn't a normal knock, but a sharp rap, insistent and demanding. She wasn't expecting anyone. Her first thought was that it might be Orion, but something in the back of her mind, some hidden instinct, told her it wasn't.

With a deep breath, she moved toward the door, hesitating for just a moment. She reached for the handle, but before she could turn it, a voice came from the other side—one she had not heard in what felt like forever.

"Elara."

Her stomach dropped. The voice was low, but familiar. The last time she'd heard it, it had been filled with anger, with bitterness—betrayal.

Jonas.

Her heart clenched painfully at the sound of his name. It had been weeks since she last saw him, weeks since she had allowed herself to think about the man she used to call her best friend. The man who had once been her anchor, her support. And now? Now, everything between them was broken, shattered by lies, secrets, and unspoken truths.

"Elara," Jonas repeated, his voice softer this time. "Please, open the door."

For a moment, she just stood there, her hand still gripping the doorknob. She didn't know what to do. Didn't know what to say. She should have been angry, should have slammed the door in his face and never looked back. But something in her—the small, vulnerable part of her that still cared—was aching to know why he was here, what had brought him back to her.

With a sigh, she turned the handle. The door creaked open, revealing Jonas standing in the hallway, his dark eyes shadowed, his expression tight. He hadn't changed much in the time they'd been apart. Same scruffy hair, same intense gaze. But now, there was a distance between them, like a rift that couldn't be bridged.

He didn't step forward. Instead, he just stood there, his gaze flicking to her face before dropping to the floor. His voice was quiet, almost hesitant.

"I need to talk to you."

Elara crossed her arms, a defensive gesture. "About what, Jonas?"

He met her eyes then, and there was something there—something unsettling. His expression was torn, as if he was wrestling with something he didn't know how to say.

"About everything," he said. "About what happened between us. About…" He trailed off, glancing over his shoulder as if making sure no one was watching. "About what's going to happen next."

Her breath caught in her throat, a knot forming in her chest. What's going to happen next? She felt like she was already drowning in things she couldn't control, things she couldn't fix.

"You're going to have to be more specific, Jonas," she said, trying to keep her voice steady, trying to mask the panic that was rising in her chest.

Jonas sighed deeply, stepping into the apartment without waiting for an invitation. He moved past her, his presence filling the small space, making her feel small and vulnerable.

"Elara," he said again, his voice raw. "I never meant to hurt you."

The words hit her harder than she expected. They weren't just an apology—they were genuine, laced with the kind of regret she hadn't heard from him in so long. She felt the sting of those words, the way they pierced the wall she had carefully built around her heart.

"I know," she whispered, her voice shaking. "But you did."

Jonas's shoulders slumped, and for a moment, he looked like the man she used to know. The man who used to be so sure of himself, so full of promise. But now? Now, there was only brokenness. And Elara didn't know if she could ever piece them back together.

"I was wrong," he said softly. "I was stupid. I should have trusted you."

But then he met her gaze, and Elara saw it—the truth he hadn't been able to tell her before. Something flickered in his eyes, something she didn't want to believe.

"I didn't tell you everything," Jonas said.

She didn't move. Didn't even breathe.

"What do you mean?" Her voice was barely a whisper, the air thick with the weight of his words.

Jonas looked at her for a long, painful moment. Then he took a deep breath and exhaled slowly.

"Elara," he said, his voice breaking, "the prophecy… it's not just about you. It's about all of us."

Her heart skipped. "What? What do you mean?"

"I'm not just your friend, Elara," Jonas said, stepping closer to her, his gaze searching her face for understanding. "I'm part of this too. I've always been part of it."

Her pulse quickened, her mind spinning. She stepped back, shaking her head. "No. You don't make sense."

"I didn't want you to know," Jonas said urgently, his voice desperate. "But the prophecy, it's been in the bloodlines of our families for centuries. I didn't know until it was too late. Until I started seeing the signs. Until the shadow came after you."

Elara's breath caught in her throat. "The shadow? What

shadow?"

Jonas stepped closer, his face inches from hers now. "Lucien. He's not just after you. He's after both of us."

Elara's knees nearly buckled beneath her. Lucien. The name was a dark whisper in her mind. The one who had come for her, who had promised her power—and more. And now, Jonas was telling her it was all part of something bigger—something she had never been prepared for.

Her thoughts scattered, but the one thing that stood clear in her mind was the question she had asked herself ever since Lucien's visit.

Who could she trust?

Eight

The Celestial Hunt

The sound of waves crashing against the shore had always been comforting to Elara. The rhythmic pulsing of the ocean was a constant companion in her life, a lullaby that soothed her restless thoughts. But tonight, as she stood at the edge of the cliff overlooking the darkened waters, the sound felt like an eerie warning.

The air was thick, oppressive, and the sky above seemed stretched, as though the stars themselves were retreating from her, hiding in the folds of clouds that hovered like a weight above the town. There was something unnatural about the night. Something wrong.

She glanced over her shoulder at the lighthouse. The beam of light that had once guided ships safely into harbor had long since gone dark, its glass shattered and its mechanism seized.

Now, the lighthouse was nothing but an abandoned relic, a hollow shell of its former self. Yet Elara couldn't shake the feeling that it was more than just a forgotten building—it was a watchtower, a sentinel in the shadows.

Elara turned back toward the cliff's edge. She could feel Orion's presence behind her, his steady gaze on her, but he didn't say anything. He hadn't said much in the past few days, and Elara couldn't decide whether that silence was comforting or suffocating.

"I'm not sure I'm ready for this," she murmured, her voice barely rising above the wind.

Orion's footsteps were almost silent as he moved to stand beside her, his gaze fixed on the horizon. "You don't have to be ready," he said, his voice low, like the rumble of distant thunder. "None of us are. But it's happening, Elara. And we have to face it."

The words seemed to hang in the air, weighty with something she hadn't fully understood until now. She wanted to ask more questions, to beg him to explain what was happening, but the fear that clutched at her chest tightened. She had no words left. All she could do was stand there, her body tense, her thoughts spinning in circles.

The hunt was about to begin.

"Do you ever feel like we're being watched?" she asked suddenly, the question escaping before she could stop herself.

Orion turned to her, his dark eyes piercing, searching her face for some hidden meaning. For a moment, it felt like he could see through her, reading every thought, every fear, but then his expression softened, and he sighed.

"All the time," he said. "I think it's why I'm always looking over my shoulder."

Elara swallowed, her heart racing as she felt the invisible eyes on her once more. It wasn't just Lucien anymore. She didn't know who, but something was tracking them—and the sensation was too real to ignore.

The air shifted, cold and biting, and Elara's stomach lurched as a shiver ran through her. She glanced toward the street below.

"I don't like it," she whispered.

Orion's hand found hers, warm and solid against the chill of the night. She didn't pull away.

"We can't afford to be afraid now," he said, his grip tightening slightly. "We're too far in. We can't go back."

Her heart hammered in her chest. It wasn't just fear. It was desperation—a need to understand, to survive.

And in that moment, she felt the pull between them again, stronger than ever. It was the same magnetic force that had drawn her to him from the beginning. But now, the bond was more than just a connection; it was a lifeline, a tether between them, and she was terrified that if she let go, she would fall.

But just as quickly, the feeling faded. The tension in the air sharpened, and Elara couldn't shake the feeling that something was coming—something she wouldn't be able to fight.

"We have to go," Orion said suddenly, his voice urgent, snapping her out of her thoughts. "Now."

Before Elara could protest, he pulled her away from the cliff's edge, guiding her quickly toward the road that led back into town.

"What is it?" she asked, her pulse quickening.

"Something's close." Orion's voice was tight, every word clipped with a sense of urgency. "Too close."

They hurried through the winding streets, the silence around them growing deeper, more suffocating. The streetlights flickered, casting long shadows across the road. Elara's breath came in sharp, ragged bursts, the cold air biting at her skin, but the closer they got to town, the heavier the air became. It was like walking through thickening fog, each step weighed down by an unseen presence.

They reached the edge of the town, where the buildings became sparse and the road grew dark. There, in the shadows of the trees, Elara saw the figure.

A man, tall and imposing, standing at the far side of the street, his back turned toward them. But something about the way he stood—the stillness in his posture—struck her with unease.

Elara's heart skipped.

Orion must have sensed it too, because he stopped, his grip on her wrist tightening.

"Stay behind me," he ordered, his voice low, a warning laced with something raw.

Elara nodded, though her chest tightened with uncertainty. She didn't like being left behind. She didn't like not knowing what was going to happen next. But she trusted Orion's instincts more than her own.

The figure turned, slowly, as if he were aware of their presence. And when his gaze locked onto hers, Elara felt a cold shiver snake down her spine. His eyes weren't human—they couldn't be. They were dark, like obsidian, swirling with shadows that seemed to shift and move, as though they were alive.

"Elara," the figure said, his voice smooth and cold, like the edge of a blade. "It's time."

Her blood ran cold.

Orion stepped forward, blocking her from the figure's gaze. "You're not welcome here," he said, his voice hard, dangerous.

The man didn't flinch. He didn't even blink. He just stood there, a silent presence, like a shadow that had slipped through the cracks of reality.

"You can't stop this," the figure said, his lips curling into a smile that didn't reach his eyes. "Not now. Not ever."

The air grew even colder. Elara could feel the tension building, thick and suffocating, and then—without warning—the figure lunged forward.

But Orion was faster.

He moved with a speed that was almost unnatural, his body a blur as he caught the figure's wrist mid-air and threw him back with a force that made the ground tremble.

Elara gasped, her heart racing, as the man's body slammed into the ground, but even as he lay there, he didn't move. He just… watched.

Orion stood between them, his chest rising and falling with heavy breaths, his body taut with the energy of the confrontation. "This ends now."

But the man only smiled again, a smile that was too cold, too knowing.

"I'm not the one you should be worried about," the figure said. "You've only just begun to realize what's coming. The hunt has only just started."

With that, he vanished into the shadows.

Orion turned toward Elara, his face grim, his eyes stormy with unspoken emotions. He reached for her, his hand hovering near her shoulder but not quite touching.

"Elara," he said, his voice low, filled with something like regret. "It's too late. We can't outrun this. We can't hide anymore."

The weight of his words sank into her chest, heavy and unyielding. They were out of time.

The hunt was beginning—and they were both its prey.

Nine

A Star's Desperate Plea

The sun had long since dipped below the horizon, leaving the world cloaked in shadows. Elara paced across the living room of her apartment, the wooden floors creaking beneath her feet as her mind churned with confusion, fear, and something darker. The moment the figure had disappeared into the night, everything had shifted. The air had grown heavier, thick with the promise of something inevitable—something that had been creeping closer ever since the star had fallen from the sky.

She could still feel it—the pull.

It was the kind of presence that gnawed at the edges of her sanity, as though every fiber of her being was tuned to the wrong frequency. The bond between her and Orion was unbreakable, but now, she wasn't sure if that bond was her salvation—or her doom. The more she tried to fight it, the more unstoppable it felt.

Orion had been distant ever since their confrontation with the mysterious figure in the streets. His silences had deepened, his movements sharper, as though he were holding back some part of himself, hiding from her, from the truth.

And she could feel it—the distance between them growing.

She stopped pacing and turned toward the window, her breath fogging the glass. Below her, the town seemed too quiet, the streets empty, the ocean beyond eerily still. She had always found comfort in the solitude of Solace Bay, in the peaceful rhythm of life that seemed to flow beneath the surface. But now, the quiet felt oppressive, suffocating. There was a tension in the air, as though the world itself was holding its breath.

Her thoughts were interrupted by the sound of the door opening. She turned, expecting Orion, but instead, it was Jonas.

Her stomach clenched.

She hadn't seen him since their last conversation—the revelation that he was tied to the prophecy, that he had known things he hadn't told her. She had been too angry, too hurt to even process what he'd said, but now, with everything unraveling around her, the anger felt like a distant echo.

Jonas stepped into the room, his face drawn, his eyes shadowed with worry. He was more disheveled than usual, his clothes wrinkled, his hair tousled as if he had been running.

"Elara," he said quietly, his voice almost apologetic. "I need to talk to you."

She crossed her arms, her gaze wary. "About what? More secrets?"

Jonas flinched at the bitterness in her voice, but he didn't back down. "It's not like that," he said, his hands raised in a placating gesture. "I'm here because I need you to understand something. Something I didn't have the courage to tell you before."

Elara took a step back, her heart beating harder in her chest. She didn't know if she could trust him anymore. The truth— whatever it was—felt like a weight on her chest, and Jonas was part of that weight. Part of the reason she couldn't breathe.

"Go on," she said, her voice tight, "I'm listening."

Jonas hesitated, then closed the distance between them, his eyes meeting hers with an intensity that sent a shiver down her spine.

"I've been lying to you, Elara," he said, his voice low, almost a whisper. "Not just about the prophecy, but about my involvement in everything. About what I know."

She blinked, her stomach twisting. The words didn't make sense. "What do you mean?"

"The prophecy—it's not just about you and me. It's about all of us," Jonas continued. His hands shook slightly, and he clenched them into fists as if he were trying to steady himself. "The star didn't fall just for you. It was meant to fall for someone else. Someone who was supposed to control it, to wield its power, and that person is—"

He stopped abruptly, as though something had caught in his throat. Elara's pulse quickened. She could feel the weight of his words before he even spoke them.

"The star chose you, Elara," he said finally, his voice breaking, "but the truth is, it wasn't just some random fall from the sky. It was the culmination of a thousand years of design. The star chose you because you were meant to be its anchor. But the cost of that power… is more than I could have imagined."

Elara's heart stopped. She wanted to scream, to demand answers, but all she could do was stand there, frozen, as his words sank into her chest like shards of glass. The star didn't just fall for her. She wasn't just some innocent bystander in all of this. She was part of a plan, a cosmic design that she didn't understand, and that thought made her feel like she was losing control of her own life.

"And Orion?" she whispered, her voice barely audible.

Jonas's face darkened, and for the first time, Elara saw something she hadn't expected—regret.

"He's not just a protector, Elara," Jonas said, his voice tight. "He's been watching over you because he's tied to the prophecy too. He's the one who's supposed to stop you from fulfilling it."

Her heart skipped, the words cutting through her like ice. "What?"

Jonas stepped closer, his hand reaching out as if to steady her, but Elara took a step back.

"He's the one who's been keeping you from realizing what you're really capable of. He's been preventing you from embracing what's coming. You're not just the vessel for the star's power, Elara. You're the one who will decide whether it remains or destroys everything."

The room seemed to spin around her. The weight of his words crushed her, suffocating her. She could feel the space between her and Jonas growing, a rift forming that she didn't know how to bridge. She had trusted him, believed in him, and now—now it felt like she didn't know him at all.

"What are you trying to say, Jonas?" she asked, her voice trembling. "What exactly does that mean for me?"

His eyes were filled with something she couldn't quite place— fear, guilt, and something else that made her stomach churn.

"It means," Jonas said, his voice breaking with the weight of it all, "that everything you thought you knew was a lie. The star was never meant to be a gift. It was meant to destroy. It was never meant to give power—it was meant to consume."

Elara's breath hitched, her head spinning. She shook her head, unable to process the full extent of what he was saying. "No, I don't believe you. You're wrong."

"I'm not," Jonas said, his voice pleading. "The prophecy—everything—is a curse, not a blessing. And now… now, we have to stop it before it consumes everything. Before it consumes you."

Elara stumbled back, her hands trembling as she pressed them against her chest. "How do we stop it?" she asked, her voice cracking.

Jonas stepped closer, his expression softening, but there was something in his eyes—something that made her take a step back.

"I don't know, Elara," he whispered. "I don't know if we can. But you have to choose. You have to decide whether you'll accept it—or whether you'll destroy it before it destroys you."

Before she could respond, a cold shiver ran through her. She heard a sound—the whisper of a movement behind her. Elara turned slowly, but by the time she could react, the door had already swung open.

Orion stood in the doorway, his face unreadable, his eyes dark with something like pain.

"Elara," he said softly, stepping into the room, his gaze flicking briefly to Jonas. "I heard everything."

Elara's heart stopped in her chest.

Jonas had spoken the truth. And now, she was caught.

In the middle of a cosmic war that was beyond her understanding, with the very fate of the universe hanging in the balance.

And for the first time, Elara realized that she had no idea what the future held—or if she was even strong enough to face it.

Ten

Fall

The walls of Elara's apartment felt like they were closing in on her. Every corner, every shadow, seemed to pulse with an unnatural tension, as if the very air was charged with electricity. She stood by the window, her gaze drifting over the distant ocean, the dark expanse stretching out before her like a vast, unknowable void. The waves crashed relentlessly against the cliffs, their rhythmic pounding the only sound in the otherwise oppressive silence.

Behind her, the conversation with Jonas still hung in the air, the words echoing like a distant drumbeat. The prophecy. The curse. The star had fallen not to bestow power but to consume everything in its wake. It was more than just a force of nature—it was an unstoppable destiny, one she had been unwillingly pulled into. And now… now the decision rested with her.

Embrace it or destroy it. There was no middle ground.

Elara's heart pounded in her chest, the weight of that choice suffocating her. Every time she closed her eyes, she saw the faces of the people she loved—her parents, her friends, the ones who had always counted on her. She had never asked for this, never chosen to be the anchor of a falling star, and yet here she was, standing at the precipice of something that could either save or destroy everything.

A soft creak of the floorboards behind her pulled her from her thoughts. She turned quickly, and her breath caught in her throat when she saw Orion standing in the doorway. His dark eyes were shadowed, his jaw clenched in that way that made her stomach tighten.

"Elara…" His voice was barely above a whisper, thick with emotion that he was clearly struggling to contain.

She opened her mouth to speak, to say something—anything—but the words caught in her throat. The pull between them, the connection that had started as a flicker of attraction, had become something far more complicated. The kiss they had shared, the moments of silence between them, had woven their fates together in ways she couldn't escape.

He stepped forward, his eyes never leaving hers. "You heard everything, didn't you?"

She nodded, though she wasn't sure if he was asking about the conversation with Jonas or something more. Her chest felt tight, as if the truth they were dancing around was too much for her to process all at once. The very idea that Orion, the person she had trusted, could be hiding something from her—something as important as the prophecy—hurt more than she had expected.

"I didn't want to tell you," he said, his voice strained. "I didn't want to burden you with all of this." He gestured vaguely, as though the entire weight of the world was on his shoulders. "But I'm not the one who gets to decide what happens next. Neither are you, Elara."

Her heart raced, and she had to bite back the urge to shout, to demand answers. The anger that had been building in her chest finally burst through the surface.

"Then who is?" she snapped, her voice harsh. "Who gets to decide what happens to me? You? Jonas? The universe?" Her chest tightened with the frustration of feeling trapped—trapped by a fate she had never asked for, trapped by a destiny that felt like it was already written in the stars.

Orion took a step closer, his eyes searching her face with an intensity that made her skin tingle. He didn't speak for a long moment, and when he did, his voice was softer, more vulnerable than she had ever heard it.

"I'm not trying to control you," he said, almost pleading. "But I don't want to lose you. You have no idea how much is at stake."

The words struck her like a punch to the gut. She hadn't

considered the possibility that he was afraid too—that the man who had always been so strong, so composed, could be as terrified as she was.

"Elara, we can't outrun this," he continued, his voice quiet but urgent. "I've been running for centuries, trying to keep the prophecy from happening. Trying to keep the star from claiming its rightful anchor. And I failed. I didn't think it was going to be you. I didn't think the bond between us would be so powerful."

She swallowed hard, the weight of his words sinking deep into her chest. The bond. That strange, undeniable connection between them. It was the only thing that had kept her from completely falling apart over the last few days. And yet, it was also the thing that had trapped her in a web of inescapable fate.

"Elara, we have to stop this. We have to stop it before it destroys everything we care about." His voice was raw now, filled with emotion he couldn't hide. "I can't—" He broke off, his voice faltering for a moment before he cleared his throat. "I can't lose you, Elara. Not like this. Not because of this prophecy."

Her heart twisted in her chest at the pain in his words. She knew he was right. She could feel the danger closing in around them both, the weight of the star's curse pressing down on them like a storm. But there was no escape from it. There was no escaping the choices they had to make.

She stepped forward, her heart pounding as she reached out to touch his arm. "I don't want to lose you either," she whispered, the words barely audible. Her fingers brushed against his skin, and the heat from his body seemed to burn into her.

For a moment, they just stood there, facing each other, the world around them falling away. The distance between them—the emotional gulf that had opened up in the wake of the prophecy— seemed to close, just for a heartbeat. She wanted to believe that they could overcome it. That love could be enough to break the chains of fate.

But deep down, she knew the truth.

"Orion," she whispered, her voice trembling with the weight of the decision that lay before them. "How do we stop it?"

He didn't respond immediately. Instead, he reached for her hand, pulling her closer, his grip firm and comforting. His eyes searched hers, his lips parted as if he were about to say something—but then he faltered, the words catching in his throat.

"I don't know," he said quietly, the admission cutting through the air. "I thought I did. I thought I had it figured out, but it's… it's all so much bigger than we thought."

Her chest tightened at his words. The uncertainty in his voice unsettled her. She had always believed in Orion's strength, in his unwavering certainty. But now, with the weight of the prophecy pressing down on them both, she realized that even he didn't have all the answers.

"Then what are we supposed to do?" she asked, her voice barely above a whisper.

He didn't answer right away. Instead, he looked at her—looked at her like she was the only thing in the world worth saving, worth fighting for. His gaze softened, and for the first time since this all began, Elara saw a flicker of something she hadn't expected: hope.

"I don't know how to stop it, Elara," he said, his voice thick with emotion. "But I'm not giving up on you. I'm not giving up on us. Not now. Not ever."

And in that moment, everything seemed to shift. The weight of the decision still pressed on her shoulders, but now, with Orion's hand holding hers, with the heat of his body so close to hers, she realized that she wasn't alone.

For better or worse, they were in this together.

And as much as the future terrified her, as much as the prophecy loomed over them like a shadow, Elara knew one thing for sure:

She would face it—with Orion at her side.

Eleven

Echoes

E lara didn't know what time it was when she woke, only that the night felt wrong. The silence was oppressive, thick with an intensity she couldn't escape. It was like the entire world was holding its breath, waiting for something to happen.

She pushed the blankets away and sat up, her head spinning as she tried to focus on the dimly lit room around her. The faint hum of the city drifted through the open window, the air cool and crisp with the salty tang of the ocean. But the sound was distant, muffled, as though the world was slipping away from her.

Elara didn't feel like she belonged in this space anymore. The walls of her apartment had become too familiar, too constraining, as if they were closing in on her. She didn't belong here. She didn't belong in a life that had been stolen from her, swept away by forces she didn't understand.

A cold gust of wind cut through the room, lifting the curtain near the window and making her shiver. The breeze was sharp against her skin, a reminder of the strange pull she'd felt ever since the star had fallen, ever since she had touched it. The bond between her and Orion had grown stronger, their fates irrevocably linked, and with it came a sense of both power and danger that lingered in her bones.

She stood, still groggy, and walked to the window, her bare feet sinking into the cold hardwood. The night beyond the glass was a vast, endless sea of darkness, the stars barely visible in the haze of a storm that was beginning to gather. The moon was obscured by thick clouds, leaving only the faintest light to guide her eyes.

But something—someone—was out there.

Elara's breath hitched, a sudden chill running down her spine. She wasn't sure if it was instinct or something deeper, something cosmic, but she knew without looking that she wasn't alone. Her pulse quickened, and she spun around, half-expecting to find Orion standing behind her, his presence solid and reassuring. But the room was empty, silent except for the sound of her own ragged breath.

Something was wrong.

There was a shift in the air, an energy she couldn't name. It thrummed beneath her skin, a subtle vibration that made her heart race, as if the universe itself had changed direction. The air had become thick, charged with an intensity that made her feel like she was about to be swept away by a storm.

She stepped toward the door, the wood creaking beneath her feet. Every step she took felt like it was pushing her deeper into something inevitable. She hesitated at the threshold, the soft thud of her heart drowning out the sound of her breath. The streetlights outside flickered in the distance, casting eerie shadows along the cobblestone streets. The city seemed to be sleeping, unaware of the darkness that was creeping closer, inch by inch.

The door creaked open, and Elara stepped out into the cool night. She wrapped her cardigan tighter around her shoulders as the wind picked up, its gusts pushing against her as though it were trying to steer her in a particular direction. But she couldn't see it—the reason she felt the pull, the presence just beyond her grasp.

She stepped carefully down the stairs, every movement deliberate, every step calculated. The shadows around her seemed to stretch longer than they should, the buildings looming over her like giants. She felt small, vulnerable, yet the pull—the call—was undeniable.

It wasn't until she reached the street that she saw him.

Orion stood at the end of the alleyway, his dark silhouette barely visible in the dim light. He was motionless, watching her with an intensity that seemed to burn through the darkness. His figure was framed by the shadows, the sharp angles of his body outlined against the faint glow of the streetlamp.

For a moment, she just stared at him, her heart in her throat. She hadn't expected him to be here. She hadn't expected to see him like this—so far removed from the man she had come to rely on, the man who had been her guide, her protector, her anchor.

But there was something different about him tonight. He wasn't just standing there. His presence felt heavy, like a storm was brewing beneath his skin. His eyes, though, they were still the same—dark, intense, full of emotions he wasn't sharing.

"Elara," he said softly, his voice low but clear. "You shouldn't be out here."

His words didn't quite reach her. Instead, her gaze lingered on him, trying to piece together the truth of what was happening. He looked the same, but there was a distance in his eyes now, a wall that hadn't been there before. It made her chest tighten, her heart breaking all over again.

"I felt something," she said, her voice trembling. She didn't need to explain. She didn't need to say the words. He knew. He always knew.

Orion nodded slowly, his eyes never leaving hers. "The hunting has begun," he said, his voice barely a whisper in the wind. "They're coming for you."

The words were simple, but they carried a weight Elara wasn't prepared for. The air around them seemed to grow heavier, the darkness pressing in. It wasn't just the threat of Lucien anymore. There were others, beings who were drawn to the star's power, to the anchor it had created. And now, they were hunting—hunting for her.

"You don't have to do this," Elara said, stepping closer, her heart racing. "You don't have to be part of this." She reached out to him, the warmth of his presence a lifeline she desperately needed.

But when Orion spoke, it was as if he were speaking from a distance, his voice cold and distant. "I'm already too deep in it, Elara. We both are."

Her breath caught in her throat. The words stung, but they didn't shock her. The truth had been sitting at the edges of her thoughts, waiting to be acknowledged. She had known for some time that they were both bound to the prophecy, but hearing him say it—hearing him accept it—made her feel more alone than she had ever felt in her life.

"Orion," she whispered, taking another step toward him, but the distance between them seemed to stretch, as if the world itself was forcing them apart. "Please. I don't want this."

He looked at her then, his eyes flickering with something soft— something vulnerable. But just as quickly, it was gone.

"I know," he said. "But the star has already chosen. And we don't get to choose how it ends."

Elara's heart slammed in her chest. She felt the fear, the desperation building inside her, but there was something else too—something deep in her gut that told her this wasn't the end. It couldn't be.

She reached for him then, desperate to bridge the gap between them. Her hand brushed against his, the touch sending a shock of electricity through her. She could feel his warmth, feel his pulse, but it wasn't enough. It wasn't enough to erase the uncertainty that stretched between them like a chasm.

Orion reached for her hand, but before their fingers could fully entwine, a sudden blast of energy surged through the air, knocking them both backward.

Elara gasped, her body thrown off balance. She looked up, her heart racing, and saw it—the shadow.

It was tall, featureless, its shape shifting with an unnatural fluidity. It had no face, no identity—just darkness, pure and consuming, moving toward them like a storm.

And then Elara realized—it wasn't alone.

More figures emerged from the shadows, surrounding them, closing in on all sides. They were fast, too fast, their movements too fluid to be human. They moved in unison, as if they were part of a greater collective, something ancient and terrifying.

"Elara!" Orion shouted, his voice thick with panic. "Run!"

But she didn't run. She couldn't. The darkness was everywhere, and as the figures closed in, Elara felt the weight of the star pulsing in her veins—its energy was calling to her, beckoning her to embrace it, to fight back. But she didn't know how.

Before she could make a move, the shadows surged forward, and the world went black.

Twelve

The Heart of the Storm

The darkness enveloped them, suffocating and complete. Elara's chest heaved with panic, but she couldn't move—couldn't think. The shadows closed around her like tendrils, twisting and writhing like they were alive. The sound of her breath, loud and ragged in her ears, was the only thing she could focus on. It was like the world had gone silent, like nothing existed outside her current space.

But even in the suffocating dark, she could still feel **it**. The pull. The energy. The **star**.

It burned in her veins, and the power thrummed in her body. It was overwhelming, filling her, pushing against her ribs, demanding to be released. For a moment, Elara thought she might drown in it—drown in the force of what she had become—what she was **meant** to become.

"Elara, listen to me."

Orion's voice sliced through the dark, sharp and urgent. The sound was like a rope thrown into the abyss, pulling her back, grounding reality, slipping further away.

"Elara." His voice was closer now but still distant like he was trapped somewhere beyond her reach.

"Orion…" She whispered his name, the word almost **lost** in the shadow, but she felt it anyway. The call of his voice, the steady force that had always been her anchor, was all she had left.

She tried to move, but the shadows were too thick and **gripping**. They wrapped around her limbs like cold hands, pulling her into the void. She gasped, struggling against the pull, but it was as though the darkness was alive, feeding off her fear and growing stronger with every heartbeat.

"Elara, you have to fight it," Orion's voice urged, softer now, full of desperation she hadn't heard before. "You have to *control* it."

Control it.

The words resonated in her chest, and a wave of **clarity** crashed over her. She had always known it, deep down—**she had the power**. The bond had tied her to the star, but it wasn't just about the star's will. She was the one with the **choice**. The star's power surged through her, but she could bend it, shape it. She had the strength to keep it from consuming her.

With that thought, the shadows recoiled. It wasn't a physical force but something more primal, more instinctual. The darkness seemed to hesitate as if it could sense her change. The air shifted, and she could breathe again, the suffocating weight lifting slightly. She could feel the power surging within her, but it was no longer a force of destruction. It was a part of her.

Orion's hands found hers in the dark, his fingers gripping her with an urgency she hadn't seen before. "Elara, please." His voice trembled, a crack in his notypicallyyomposed tone. "I don't know how much longer I can hold it back."

His words hit her like a physical blow. There was something in how he said it—a **warning**, an unspoken truth that she hadn't fully understood until now.

Something was coming. And they were both running out of time.

"Elara, you have to choose. *Now*."

His grip tightened around her, and she realized, with a shuddering breath, that he wasn't just holding onto her physically—he was holding onto the last piece of **humanity** she had left. The world around them was crumbling, and the weight of the decision pressing down on her felt suffocating.

She had to **choose**.

At that moment, Elara knew what she had to do. She couldn't let the power of the star **destroy** her—not again. It wasn't just about the prophecy anymore; it was about who she was, about what she was willing to fight for. It was about **herself**.

The shadows began to shift again, creeping closer, but this time, they were different. They were no longer a force of destruction; now, they were **subject** to her will. The power within her wasn't just a tool to fight with—it was a **part of her**, an extension of her soul.

"Elara," Orion breathed, his voice low and filled with awe. "You're doing it. You're controlling it."

Her heart raced in her chest as she focused, pushing against the darkness, shaping it, bending it to her will. The shadows wavered, their tendrils faltering under her power. The world around them seemed to ripple, and for a moment, everything felt **still**.

Then, the shadows collapsed.

Elara gasped, the sudden release of tension making her dizzy. The power inside her surged, and she had to fight to **contain** it, to keep it from spiraling out of control. The bond between her and the star pulsed within her, but now, she **controlled** it.

Orion stepped forward, his face illuminated by the faintest glow, his eyes wide with something that could only be described as wonder.

"Elara," he said, his voice raw, filled with disbelief. "You did it."

She looked at him, feeling the energy coursing through her body, but there was no triumph in her gaze—only exhaustion. The shadows had been banished, but the battle was far from over.

"I don't know if I can keep this up," she whispered, the words trembling in her throat. "I don't know how much longer I can control it."

Orion's gaze softened, and he reached out to gently cup her face, his touch warm and grounding. His hand trembled slightly, but he didn't let go.

"You won't have to," he murmured. "Not alone. You're not alone in this, Elara."

His words were like a lifeline thrown to her in the storm's chaos, and she clung to them. She had been so afraid—afraid of losing herself, of being consumed by the star's power, of being unable to find a way out of the **inevitable** fate she had been thrust into. But in Orion's eyes, she saw something different. She saw the possibility of **freedom and** that they could rewrite the prophecy together.

For a brief moment, everything fell silent. There was no storm, no dark forces surrounding them. The two of them, standing in the stillness, connected in a way they had never been before.

And then the moment shattered.

A sudden, deafening sound ripped through the air, the **crack of something breaking**, and Elara stumbled, her legs buckling beneath her. She gasped for air, her mind swirling, trying to keep the energy within her from spiraling out of control.

"Elara!" Orion's voice was panicked, and she felt his hands on her shoulders, steadying her. "What's happening?"

She couldn't answer. The power inside her—**the star**—was twisting, turning, and she couldn't understand it. It was no longer just the pull of the prophecy. It was something darker, something **demanding**.

The sky above them seemed to ripple, the clouds darkening,

and a bright light flashed across the horizon, blinding her.

For a brief moment, Elara thought she saw **something** in the light—something celestial, something **alive**. The stars seemed to shimmer and twist as though they were pulling toward her, drawn to the energy within her.

And then it came.

A **whisper**. Not a voice, but a sensation that flooded her mind. A knowledge.

"The end is near."

The words were like a prophecy, a **warning** wrapped in a soundless scream.

Orion gripped her tighter, his face pale with concern, but Elara felt something shift within her. The star's energy was no longer a force of destruction but a **calling**—a deep, primal call to **action**.

She wasn't the anchor. She was the key.

Her heart pounded as the realization washed over her. The end was near, but not just for her. It was for them all.

She had the power to decide the fate of the universe. The only question was—**would she survive it?**

www.ingramcontent.com/pod-product-compliance
Lightning Source LLC
LaVergne TN
LVHW051937060726
842528LV00011B/2450